FREEZE DRYING FOR BEGINNERS

How to Freeze Dry and Preserve Nutrient Dense Food Safely at Home.

1000 Days of Tasty Recipes and Log Book Included.

TABLE OF CONTENTS

INTRODUCTION.. 5

CHAPTER 1: FREEZE DRYING BASICS................................ 10

SCIENCE BEHIND FREEZE-DRYING... 22

FREEZE DRYING WITH A FREEZE DRYER MACHINE 28

PREPARATION OF FREEZE-DRIED FOOD 33

USING A MACHINE TO FREEZE DRY 36

FREEZE DRYING WITHOUT A MACHINE 38

HOW TO FREEZE-DRY FOOD WITH DRY ICE............................ 39

FREEZE-DRYING FOOD USING LIQUID NITROGEN.................... 41

INSTRUCTIONS FOR STORING FREEZE-DRIED FOOD 42

CHAPTER 2: FREEZING - THE MOST EFFECTIVE METHOD
TO FREEZE DRY FOOD... 45

THE FREEZING PROCEDURE 52

THINGS TO CONSIDER BEFORE FREEZING YOUR FOOD 57

MAINTAINING QUALITY WHEN FREEZING 65

TOOLS AND EQUIPMENT... 67

FREEZING MEAT AT HOME 74

THAWING 90

FLASH FREEZING 94

HOW TO PROPERLY STORE FROZEN FOOD 108

CHAPTER 3: RECIPES TO HELP YOU GET STARTED WITH
YOUR FREEZE-DRYING PROCESS 115

    1. TERIYAKI MARINADE 116

    2. TOMATO PASTE... 118

    3. CHICKEN BONE BROTH.................................. 121

    4. SPINACH AND PARMESAN FRITTATAS............ 124

    5. VEGAN SOUP.. 126

CONCLUSION..129

INTRODUCTION

We have numerous options for food preservation methods to extend the shelf-life of food consumed at home or in your food business. You can use cooling, freezing, canning, sugaring, salting, and even vacuum packaging. Furthermore, food preservation experts constantly research new techniques to expand our options.

We must prioritize the safest food preservation techniques, which have been learned through centuries of trial and error, as these will help us preserve the quality and cleanliness of stored food. The good news is that you can do it in any situation with the right instructions and resources.

Food preservation refers to the techniques used to prepare food for safe, long-term storage, whether consumed at home, in a professional kitchen or sold directly to customers. Preserved food will be safe and delicious to eat in the future because preservation techniques limit bacterial growth and other spoilage.

Food preservation is essential for three reasons:

1. Pathogenic bacteria – Pathogenic bacteria, such as E. coli, Salmonella, and other pathogens, pose a significant risk of food spoilage during long-term storage. Bacteria only require heat, moisture, and time to reproduce quickly in food, but

food preservation limits one or more of these factors, halting their proliferation.

2. To keep the food of the highest quality – Food quality degrades over time due to spoilage. In many cases, moderate spoilage does not make food unsafe to eat, but it drastically alters its flavor, texture, and appearance. Proper food preservation may preserve some of these characteristics and the nutritional value of specific foods.

3. To save money – Food is expensive both at home and at work. Ideally, you should avoid purchasing more food than you can eat. Nonetheless, various safe preservation techniques allow you to store vegetables, fruits, meat, and other foods much past their expected

expiration date, eliminating the need to discard them.

Specific food preservation techniques may be challenging to master, but once you do, you will almost certainly feel a sense of accomplishment and pride. You will also better understand food hygiene issues and best practices because many food preservation techniques require precision and care to ensure food safety. This book will discuss the best method for preserving food: freeze-drying. Let's get started without further ado.

Chapter 1:

Freeze Drying Basics

Freeze-drying is a food preservation technique that removes all fluid from a specific food without affecting its taste. Agricultural products are dried to reduce the amount of water in them. At the same time, freeze-drying is a preservation technique in which the sample material is frozen below its glass transition temperature, and then frozen water dissolves as the process pressure and temperature are reduced.

Freeze-drying is a modern dehydration technique that removes moisture efficiently while causing minor structural deformation in the product. Because of the low process enthalpy, it is a less severe thermal process degrades heat-sensitive compounds minimally while protecting thermo-liable constituents. The product is freeze-dried at low and high temperatures.

Freeze-drying requires a two-step process that starts with freezing your food. When food is frozen, it undergoes a vacuum cycle. This cycle will convert all ice gems formed during freezing into a fume. The fume is removed from the food and is safe for consumption now and in the future without losing its tone or taste.

In addition to freezing, there is an ancient method known as freeze-drying that you can use to preserve your food. Freeze-drying, contrary to what the name implies, is not the same as the methods previously discussed. Technically, freeze-drying is a type of dehydration.

The Incan empire once spanned the harsh terrain of the Andes. They thrived in that harsh, unforgiving landscape, which was bitterly cold at night but also windy and dry. They developed Chuo, a freeze-dried potato that could sustain their massive armies for years. It was created by Altiplano villagers from Peru and Bolivia's high plateaus. There are two kinds of Chuo: black and white. The former is made by freezing harvested bitter potatoes overnight and crushing them with their feet during the day to remove the skin and squeeze out the liquids until they are completely dehydrated. In contrast, the latter is made by soaking or submerging the potatoes in freezing waters of local streams and rivers and then drying them out in the sun.

Chuos are still eaten in the Andes today. Locals adore it, but the flavor is difficult for visitors to adjust to. By simply adding water, Chuos can be eaten as if you are eating freeze-dried mashed potatoes. The locals add it to other local dishes where a potato can be used, such as the local chili or aji. It can also be ground into powder to make flour that can thicken stews and soups.

The long shelf life can also save the livelihoods of locals who rely on a good harvest to survive. If the crops fail this year, they will have stored chuo to help them get by.

So, what about this method makes the food last so long? The chalk-like dehydrated potatoes of the Andes are said to rival the shelf life of modern freeze-dried food. Heat is used to extract moisture from food during dehydration. Dehydration will remove approximately 95% of the water content from the food, whereas freeze-drying will remove about 99% of the water content. As a result, your food will have a longer shelf life and taste better than your dehydrated counterparts. Despite the name, freeze-dried foods do not need to be stored in the freezer or even the refrigerator. When packaged correctly in airtight and vacuum-sealed mylar bags, freeze-dried foods can last long, even if kept in a cupboard.

Furthermore, because the water content of the food items is extracted, freeze-dried food rehydrates easily and quickly, making it the ideal way to process food that you intend to store for an extended period. Rehydrated freeze-dried food can be used in the same way as fresh food. If you freeze-dried raw bacon, rehydrate it with just a bowl of fresh potable water, and it'll be ready to cook just like regular freshly bought bacon. Cooked foods like stews, roasts, soups, and stir-fried dishes can also be freeze-dried with little flavor or quality loss. Furthermore, freeze-dried food should be consumed within four months of opening.

As a result, NASA prefers this method when packing food for our astronauts to take into space. It is delivered into space in small bags that astronauts can quickly rehydrate with just a little water. Preppers also like this method for preserving meats and other cooked foods for their bunkers and go bags because it keeps them fresh indefinitely. The disadvantage is that raw food items must be rehydrated to be consumed safely, but meals cooked before freeze-drying are generally safe to consume when opened and rehydrated. However, because it is dehydrated, it will absorb water from other sources, such as your saliva or the inside of your stomach, so that you will rehydrate the food one way or another.

In natural disasters that only last a few days without access to freshwater, freeze-dried food will be extremely useful, if not life-saving. However, in disasters where you will be without clean water for days or weeks, consumption of freeze-dried food should be limited, and water should be saved for drinking. Backpackers and climbers should also avoid freeze-dried food. Activities that cause you to sweat profusely and expend a great deal of energy dehydrate your body; furthermore, eating freeze-dried food will not only contribute to dehydration in your body but will also "back up" your gastrointestinal tract by absorbing more water as it exits your body. Bring plenty of water and electrolyte-rich drinks if you're climbing or camping with freeze-dried food to help you rehydrate properly.

When food is freeze-dried, it goes through a process known as lyophilization. Food will be chilled to temperatures well below freezing. The water content is removed when vacuum pressure is applied to the food. It is extracted as vapor, which condenses back into ice in the machine's condenser. The temperature is then gradually raised to allow the remaining moisture in the food to be extracted while retaining the structure of the food, which helps rehydrate the food in the future.

Compared to regular freezing in the freezer, rapid freezing will preserve the quality of your food the best because it produces smaller ice crystals. Because liquid nitrogen flash freezes the items, minor damage to the quality of the meats, poultry, and fish occurs, allowing them to retain their quality quite effectively. In addition, unlike regular freezing, the extremely low temperature will be able to kill any bacteria or pathogen that could cause your food to spoil.

You can also go old school and do it the Inca way, flash freezing it and leaving it to dry out in the sun, hoping for the best.

Finally, compared to dehydrating, the latter is far more cost-effective for home use. Unless you spend thousands of dollars on equipment, freeze-drying cannot be done at home. Unless you own a farm or intend to start a freeze-drying business, it is best to stick to standard freezing and dehydration.

The following are some of the reasons why people freeze dry food:

1. Frozen foods are superior to canned and dehydrated foods.

2. Freeze-drying retains nutritional value better than other drying methods, supporting consumers' desire for whole-food nutrition.

3. The freeze-drying process preserves the original raw material's color and shape, assuring consumers that they are eating natural fruits and vegetables.

4. The freeze-drying process eliminates the possibility of bacterial growth by removing the water in the product.

5. Freeze-dried foods require less time to prepare. Simply pour in some hot, boiling water, wait a few minutes, and you're ready to go.

6. Freeze-dried foods have a longer shelf life of up to 25 years.

7. Freeze-dried food is a great solution for people who cannot eat candy due to braces or dentures.

8. Freeze-dried food is a great solution for people who cannot eat candy due to sensitive teeth.

9. Freeze-dried foods are lightweight and inexpensive to transport. The food's nutritional value, flavor, and size are all preserved, and these foods can be stored for months or years. Unlike dehydrated foods, freeze-dried foods can be quickly rehydrated. Trekkers, hikers, and backpackers benefit greatly from freeze-dried foods.

10.   Freeze-dried foods can be used as emergency supplies on a rainy day.

Science Behind Freeze-Drying

The structure shrinks and deforms less when it is frozen. A vacuum pump can create a vacuum by lowering the pressure below the triple point of water and monitoring the pressure with sensors such as a capacitance manometer throughout the process. Heating plates provide the latent heat of sublimation. Using a refrigerated condenser, the vacuum pump draws sublimated vapors from the process chamber and condenses them to ice. The drying rate slows because the ice/sublimation front moves backward when ice molecules sublime.

Low pressure or vacuum slows the rate of diffusion. When ice is removed from a porous structure, the volume reduction is negligible compared to other drying methods. During drying, evaporated vapors can be recovered by condensing in a refrigerated condenser. The microscopic porous structure aids reconstitution by efficiently regaining maximum water, improving product quality, allowing for the recovery of crispy texture, and shortening the rehydration cycle time.

The shelf life of freeze-dried products containing 2% MC is about two days. The final product does not require refrigeration due to the high quality of its end products. If the resistance occurs at the mouth of the pore, pore blockage kinetic theory can be investigated to improve the quality of dried products. The drying process should maximize component retention (ascorbic acid, nutrients, vitamins), preserve nutritional and sensory values, and reduce processing time and capital costs. Freeze-drying is used for solid (fruits, vegetables, and meat) and liquid raw materials (homogenous solutions). The freeze-drying process is completed in three major stages, with no raw material pre-treatment required.

Using a plate, blast, immersion, or liquid blast freezing method, water in a sample food is frozen below its eutectic temperature. It is considered successful freezing when 95 percent of the water is converted to ice.

Freezing affects the distribution of pore size. The optimal freezing rate must be chosen because it affects the drying rate and final product quality. The eutectic point can be determined using thermal analysis techniques such as cryo-microscopy, differential scanning calorimetry, and time versus temperature curve methodologies. The freezing rate governs crystal growth and ice morphology. Slow freezing results in larger crystals, a porous structure, and an increased drying rate, damaging the product's tissues and reducing rehydration efficiency. Accelerated freezing produces small ice crystals that promote intense nucleation while permitting easy reconstitution and rapid drying.

Initial Drying

The process chamber pressure is lower (13.5 270Pa absolute) than the ice vapor pressure in the sample material to sublime ice. Conduction and radiation through the lower and upper plates provide latent sublimation heat. As a result of initial drying or ice sublimation, a dry layer forms on the top surface of the sample product. Diffusion through this partial dry layer or heat movement through the frozen and dry layers determines the drying rate. A refrigerated condenser condenses diffused vapors, and a vacuum pump is used to remove non-condensable gases. This is the longest stage of the freeze-drying process.

During initial drying, a temperature range of -20 to +20 is maintained. Heat transfer can only occur through conduction or radiation because convection lacks its medium due to the absence of air. The product is heated to a temperature below its glass transition temperature. In initial drying, the condenser temperature should be lower than the product temperature. The maximum heat should be less than its eutectic temperature, which raises the pressure difference between the condenser and the product. Heat transfer stops when the product and shelf temperatures become the same, resulting in lower system pressure and condenser temperature values due to no evaporated load. The end of initial drying can be accurately determined using comparative pressure measurement methods.

Freeze-drying preserves the nutritional value, heat-sensitive compounds, color, shape, texture, size, aroma, and flavor of agricultural products. The ongoing development of freeze-drying, as well as future aspects, make its application very feasible. The primary process parameters vary depending on the chemistry of the subjected product. Freeze-drying is an ancient technique that has evolved and continues to improve. However, freeze-drying has a high process and fixed cost. The freeze dryer freezes the product's water before applying the latent sublimation heat to sublimate the frozen water and then increasing the heat to remove any remaining water.

Freeze Drying with a Freeze Dryer Machine

If you're planning a large-scale freeze-drying empire or simply want to try freeze-drying, one of these machines might be worth investing in. A freeze-drying machine will undoubtedly be a worthwhile investment if you own a farm or a fruit farm. It is important to note that if you need to prepare food for storage quickly, having a freeze dryer in your home will not save you much time. If you want something quick and efficient, other methods are preferable. Overloading the trays and containers of a freeze dryer is not permitted. The drying time will vary between one day for thin slices of meat and fruits and three days for thicker and larger chunks of food.

To get into the deep end of freeze-drying, you must first understand that three steps must occur for a satisfying freeze-dried product to be produced. You can buy a freeze-drying machine or rig something together if you're daring by following YouTube tutorials.

Numerous resources are available to teach you how to set up a vacuum chamber in your home.

The first step in creating a DIY home freeze-drying rig is to freeze. You'll need a heavy-duty freezer that can withstand temperatures as low as -30°F or even lower. As previously stated, you can also flash freeze the items with liquid nitrogen for this stage. Second, you'll need an airtight vacuum-sealed chamber and a vacuum pump to extract moisture from your food. This second stage is known as initial drying or sublimation. Finally, there is desorption, also known as secondary drying. Attach a thermostat and a heater to the rig so that you can gradually add heat to the chamber to draw the remaining moisture out. This step is required so that you can adjust the temperature inside the chamber to repeat the sublimation process. A humidity sensor is also needed to determine whether all of the moisture has been removed from your food items.

Armed with this knowledge, you should now ask yourself a few questions before beginning your freeze-drying adventure. What are you going to do with it? Will it only be used for camping or backpacking? Do you buy bulk and plan to freeze-dry cooked items for your family's meals? Or are you a doomsday prepper preparing for the end of the world or nuclear fallout?

Whatever your reason, even a home freeze-drying machine will be an expensive purchase. It is highly preferable to consider your reasons. You don't want to spend a thousand dollars on equipment that will only be used once and collect dust in your basement or garage. Additionally, these machines are large and heavy, taking up much space in your kitchen.

One of the best ways to preserve your groceries or surplus garden harvest is to freeze-dry them. Sublimation removes water from food by converting it from a solid to a vapor or gas. Freeze-drying is one of the best ways to preserve food because it retains almost all nutritional value.

Canning and dehydrating food changes the flavor and color and reduces the nutritional content by half. Freeze-dried foods can be stored in the refrigerator, pantry, or cellar for up to 25 years. They're small and lightweight, making them ideal for quick camping meals or an emergency food supply. Most homeowners can access a home freezer and dry ice if they do not have a freeze-dryer.

Preparation of Freeze-Dried Food

Before freeze-drying your food, select the freshest options. The food should then be chopped into small pieces or bits to remove moisture. Cooked meals, on the other hand, can be frozen entirely.

If you can afford it, a freeze-dryer is an excellent option because it is explicitly designed for freeze-drying. There are numerous dryers to choose from, so make sure you get an affordable one. The advantage of these dryers is that they come with various trays for different meals.

Follow the procedures below to freeze-dry your goods. Remember to test your meals before storing them if you use this method:

1. Place your meals in the trays, ensuring they do not exceed the tray's height.
2. Place the trays in the dryer after closing the doors (Some models have two doors).
3. Freeze the food between -40 and -50 degrees Fahrenheit.
4. Allow 24 hours for the procedure to be completed.
5. After they're done, place the food in Mylar bags and seal them.

How Does a Home Freeze Dryer Work?

The following is an excerpt from "The Good, the Bad, and the Ugly of Home Freeze Drying":

- First, you get a sturdy freezer (Harvest Right units can reach -30°F or lower).
- Second, you pair it with an airtight chamber capable of maintaining a vacuum (no oxygen) at all times.
- Finally, you connect a vacuum pump powerful enough to remove zebra stripes.
- Install a heater and thermostat to cycle the temperature up and down for many hours, repeating the sublimation process.
- Fifth, connect a humidity sensor to confirm that the water has evaporated and the cycle is complete.

Many goods, such as dairy products, whole meals (hot dishes, cream-based soups, etc.), and leftovers, cannot be preserved conventionally but can be frozen at home. Fruits, vegetables, meats, and seafood can also be preserved.

Using a Machine to Freeze Dry

Freeze-drying food with a machine is about as simple as it gets. You wash the food you intend to save and cut them into smaller pieces. When the food is ready, place it on the machine's tray, turn it on, and use the machine as the manufacturer directs.

When the food has finished drying, place it in a fixed plastic pack and store it. Although drying food varieties with a machine is quick and easy, it is quite expensive.

You can expect to spend a significant amount of money. If you want to take the easier route and use this strategy to protect your food, be prepared to contribute.

People who are new to freeze-drying food benefit from having a home freezer. This is an even better option if you have a deep freezer. However, your standard home freezer will continue to work.

1. Place the food on a tray or dish after being spread out.
2. Place the tray in the freezer to freeze the food at the coldest temperature possible.
3. Allow the food to freeze for 2–3 weeks or until entirely freeze-dried.
4. After completing the procedure, store it in an airtight storage bag in your freezer or pantry.

Freeze Drying without a Machine

Freeze-drying with a machine is simple, but doing it without a machine isn't too tricky.

The primary difference between using a machine and not one is the amount of time the interaction takes. If you dry food without a machine, you should prepare it as you usually would before securing it with another method.

When the food is finished, place it on an air-drying rack so the air can completely circle it.

Place the plate in a deep cooler and leave it there. The food will immediately freeze. The food will become dry in a matter of weeks.

You will notice that the food has wholly dried by removing one piece. If the food doesn't change color as it defrosts, you'll know the interaction is finished.

How to Freeze-Dry Food with Dry Ice

Use protective equipment for this process because dry ice can burn your skin.

Place the food in a freezer bag and freeze it with dry ice. If you leave it open, the escaping air could cause your bag to explode. Pile a lot of dry ice on top of the freezer bag and leave it for 24 hours to dry. After 24 hours, the container or freezer will be filled with carbon dioxide, so do this in a well-ventilated area. Carbon dioxide inhalation in confined spaces can be fatal. If successful, frozen food must be stored in vacuum-sealed airtight containers with no moisture allowed to enter the bag.

It saves time to use dry ice instead of frozen food. This is because dry ice quickly evaporates moisture from the meal. Fill freezer bags with the food. Place the bags in the fridge. Freeze the bags for 24 hours, completely wrapped in dry ice. Remove and store the bags after they have entirely freeze-dried.

Items that are ideal for freezing with dry ice:

- Broth: Take a handful and use it for cooking or flavoring.
- Citrus juice can be used in beverages, seasonings, and dressings.
- Coffee/Tea: Use cool beverages like iced coffee and iced tea without diluting them.

- Herbs: Combine 2 cups fresh herbs and 1 cup water in a blender until smooth, then pour into trays. Frozen herbs are convenient for incorporating into cooked or pureed foods such as soups, sauces, and marinades.

Yogurt can be stored in the freezer for 2 to 3 months. You can blend it into a smoothie as a creamier alternative to ice.

Freeze-Drying Food Using Liquid Nitrogen

If you want to freeze dry items at home, another method that will undoubtedly come up when you search the internet is liquid nitrogen. Of course, liquid nitrogen quickly freezes food when it comes into contact with it. Liquid nitrogen, at -320°F, will freeze anything it comes into contact with and should be handled cautiously. Often, liquid nitrogen will be used as a faster way to bring the food to a temperature below freezing before a vacuum pump can extract all of the moisture from the food. If you don't have a drying machine, you can still flash freeze your food before storing it in the freezer with liquid nitrogen.

Instructions for Storing Freeze-Dried Food

Currently, your food options are freeze-dried. What would be a fantastic next step for you? When food sources have finished drying, place them in a plastic sack or compartment that seals.

There is no compelling reason to keep the items in the refrigerator or cooler. If all else is equal, store them in a cool place with temperatures no higher than 75°F.

This could be a root cellar, storage room, or bureau in many homes.

Food security did not appear to be this simple for many years, but we are fortunate. You can dry your food for long-term storage in just a few hours.

You can also store it for an extended period without any special requirements. You may have considered freeze-drying if you're looking for a simple way to save food.

Chapter 2:

Freezing - The Most Effective Method To Freeze Dry Food

Freezing food is a simple process that requires no special equipment, making it ideal for beginners. Prepare your vegetables by blanching or cooking them before freezing. This process inhibits enzyme activity while maintaining high quality. Blanching involves heating your vegetables and immersing them in cold water to stop cooking. Blanching time in boiling water is expected to be three minutes.

Freeze-drying appears to be an excellent method of food preservation, leading you to believe it is extremely perplexing. In any case, freeze-drying food has been around for a long time. It is straightforward and can be refined with or without a machine.

Vacuum sealing frozen products prevents ice crystal formation and can increase the shelf life of frozen items by three to five times. Non-vacuum-sealed items are rarely placed in the freezer. On the other hand, fruits can be frozen "as is" or added with a bit of sugar or antioxidants to help extend storage life and slow discoloration. If you want to freeze fruits and vegetables for long-term storage, consider freezing them on a cookie sheet and then vacuum-sealing them. This helps prevent ice crystal formation, which can increase the storage life of your frozen fruits and vegetables by up to 5 times.

Freezing is one of the most straightforward and convenient methods of food preservation and one of the oldest, along with dehydration. Before the invention of modern home appliances, communities in the far north or near mountain ranges discovered that food did not spoil in freezing temperatures. The power of cold temperatures gave rise to ice boxes (literally, metal boxes stuffed with ice), which eventually evolved into the refrigeration we have today.

Because freezing lowers the temperature of food, micro-organisms can no longer function, and enzymes act at a much slower rate. It's worth noting that I didn't say it "kills" the micro-organisms; they're still there, just not moving. Enzymes will also be present and working much slower, but they will still function, implying that decay will occur much more slowly. Because spoilage elements are still present, once an item thaws, it begins to spoil quickly.

The goal of freezing food is not only to keep it fresher for longer but also to preserve its quality. With this in mind, you should place your food in the freezer with as little air as possible. Food deteriorates due to a leak when exposed to air from outside or within the container.

You can freeze anything you can process in a jar and even more, but deciding which method to use requires weighing the benefits and drawbacks of freezing food. Freezing is ideal for seafood, berries, and other perishable produce (like broccoli). Freezing preserves much of the nutritional value, color, and texture of foods, but there are drawbacks to be aware of. A freezer has limited space; you cannot choose to freeze everything. And, unlike other methods, freezing necessitates defrosting and, in some cases, cooking. It's also difficult to transport unless you have a portable freezer.

Frozen foods, on the other hand, have a shelf life of 3 to 1 year when properly stored. When the temperature of your freezer fluctuates (due to a malfunction, power outage, or being left open for too long), the quality of the frozen items inside can suffer. If there is a prolonged rise in temperature, it is critical to check all frozen items (especially meat) to ensure that they are still frozen. If the item has completely thawed, you should prepare it within the next few days or refreeze it. Label these items with the date and the word "refrozen."

Frozen foods can last for months if properly stored. Because germs cannot develop when food is frozen, food stored in the freezer can be consumed for almost indefinite periods. However, its quality will quickly deteriorate and become unappealing, so most frozen foods should be consumed within a few months to a year.

- To freeze food securely, set the freezer to a temperature between -18°C and -22°C.

- Place food in airtight containers or freezer bags before freezing. Meat is especially prone to freezer burn and becomes unusable if not properly packaged.

- Items should be frozen only before their best-before or use-by dates.

- Never refreeze defrosted food because it allows germs to grow between thawings.

- Consume it right away or refrigerate it for up to 24 hours.

- Defrost the freezer frequently to avoid ice accumulation. You should be able to store frozen items in the refrigerator for a few hours while the freezer defrosts.

Foods should be labeled with the date they were frozen. You can check the expiration date to see if you should eat the food before it spoils. To determine the shelf life of frozen foods, use our online guide.

The Freezing Procedure

Freezing isn't rocket science; you've almost certainly done it before, but there are ways to do it better. This is how.

1. Clean Out Your Freezer

If you want to maximize your freezer and your freezing skills to the fullest, you must fi overhaul your freezer. Empty it, asses everything inside, and decide which items are old and/or will be used in a reasonable amount of time. Be honest: are you going to use everything in there? It's also fine, to begin with, an empty freezer so you can fill it with purpose. After you've emptied it, thoroughly clean it, and make sure it has a thermometer, either built into the unit or one you add.

2. Select and Prep Your Ingredients

Select the best and most fresh ingredients you can find. Fruit should be at its peak of flavor, vegetables should be young, and meats should be of the highest possible quality. Wash everything thoroughly but do not soak

ained water expands as

king food tissues and cell

ng quality. As needed, pre-

1.

our Frozen Items Into Portions

n portion things however you want if

have the proper vessels to place them in.

This allows you to freeze quantities based on how much you want to eat or serve.

Refrigerate animal proteins until ready to cut, and work in small batches as you package them to avoid contamination and quality loss.

Cut fruits and vegetables to your liking and place them in a single layer on a parchment paper-lined tray to freeze. Freeze liquid ingredients in pint or quart containers or heavy-duty resealable plastic bags. If you're freezing in a bag, seal it and place it on a rimmed baking sheet to freeze; once frozen, stack the bags to store.

4. Put Labels On Your Packages

On each package, label your items and include the date frozen. If you want, include words like "spicy," "sugar-free," or "contains nuts."

5. Change Out Your Frozen Foods

Place new freezer items in the back of the freezer and older items in the front. This policy, known as "FIFO" (first in, first out), ensures that older food is used first, reducing waste. Make a raw protein section on the bottom or separate it from other items in the freezer. This reduces the risk of cross-contamination if a meat container breaks or leaks.

However, unlike smoking or curing, freezing does not kill bacteria that can cause food to spoil. Because freezing only stops or slows bacterial growth, spoilage can still occur if your items are not appropriately frozen. To avoid this, food must be frozen quickly and kept at a temperature below 0°F at all times.

By keeping your freezer temperature at or below 0°F, you can not only stop the growth of bacteria that can cause spoilage but also reduce changes in the texture, nutritional value, and flavor of your foods.

Things To Consider Before Freezing Your Food

Arrange items in your freezer, so there is enough space between them for cold air to circulate, allowing for an even freeze—only stack items on top of each other when they are completely frozen. At the same time, avoid opening and closing your freezer multiple times daily. The constant temperature fluctuation will cause the items inside the freezer to thaw and freeze repeatedly. Even minor changes in the freezer will cause the smaller ice crystals to grow larger over time, causing further damage to the meat's cell structure and, in the long run, a softer and mushier texture. Temperature changes will also cause water to seep out of the meat, making it less juicy and healthier.

When freezing cooked meat, including the sauce, gravy, or marinade in the bag. This can also help to prevent moisture loss and freezer burn. Before storing it in the freezer, you should also allow pre-cooked food to cool to room temperature. Still, hot food takes a lot more energy to cool down and freeze, raising your electricity bill. Allowing your items to cool to room temperature slows the freezing process and helps maintain their quality.

Some loose food items, such as fruits and vegetables and lower-priced meat, can be tray-packed. Tray-packed items are first arranged in a tray to be quickly frozen so that individual pieces do not touch one another or in one thin layer that is easily broken up when frozen. Afterward, the items are collected and placed in a smaller container or bag for easier access. Berries, broccoli, chopped chicken, chicken wings, patties, and nuggets are all examples of tray-packable foods.

If you don't already have a vacuum sealer, you don't need to buy one if you're only freezing a few items for your home. It is important to note that this is not vacuum packing because you will be unable to remove all of the air from the bag. To do so, fill a large bowl halfway with water and place your meat in a resealable freezer bag. Zip it almost up until you have about a quarter-inch left open. Submerge the bag slowly in the water, slowly pulling down until all the air is pushed out and only the tip left open is above the water.

Butter and margarine can also be frozen when cut and separated by smaller pieces of parchment or baking paper. While the butter or margarine is still cool, cut it into smaller flat squares—place parchment paper between the layers and freeze.

Try to portion the items according to the number of servings you intend to use. This will keep your food from spoiling due to repeated thawing.

Because water expands when frozen, your food will do the same. To prevent leakage, give your meats some wiggle room when packing them in resealable plastic bags. Before putting your items in the fridge, ensure they are correctly labeled. This will save you significant time searching for the right items. It also reduces the time the freezer is left open while you search.

Defrost or thaw food in the refrigerator, with a tray or plate underneath to catch the juices. Food should not be left to thaw in a warm place because it will spoil. Consider the enzymes responsible for its breakdown when freezing food. These enzymes are responsible for hastening the ripening or maturing of plants and the breakdown of cellular structures in meats. If these reactions are allowed to continue, the food's color, flavor, and texture will change. To avoid this, many people blanch the food quickly or add ascorbic acid to prevent browning.

Blanching is the process of quickly immersing food in boiling water for 30 seconds to a minute, followed by rapid cooling in an ice bath. This is mainly done with vegetables, stopping and inactivating the enzymes while also killing any micro-organisms on the surface. Blanching your vegetables allows you to store them for longer periods and takes up less space in your freezer.

Chemical compounds such as ascorbic acid, also known as Vitamin C, can prevent browning on fruits typically eaten raw and thus cannot be blanched. Lemon juice can be substituted for vitamin C if it is unavailable.

The most common issue people face when it comes to meat is rancidity. Freezing meat that will be cooked in a few weeks is fine, especially if it has already been vacuum-packed and frozen. However, if you plan to store fresh meats from the butcher for an extended period, it is best to trim the excess fat and place them in an airtight wrap or a vacuum-sealed plastic bag. This extra step will also help prevent freezer burn, which is damage to meat or other food caused by moisture loss and exposure to air. While the meat is still safe to eat, it may develop dark or gray spots, and the surface may resemble leather. On the other hand, fruits and vegetables will have their water content converted into ice crystals, shriveling and drying out.

Another factor to consider is the food's texture. When water freezes, it expands, so when you freeze food, the cell walls break down or rupture as the water inside them freezes. When the food has finally thawed, it will have a softer or mushy texture. Because of their higher water content, some vegetables and fruits exhibit this effect more than meat. As a result, if you find frozen fruit chunks in your freezer, serving them while they are still partially frozen is best.

Cooking the food beforehand softens the cell walls, reducing the adverse effects. Food that is quickly frozen can produce better results. According to research, the larger the ice crystals, the longer it takes for the food to freeze. As a result, it will cause more cell damage. However, rapidly freezing the food results in smaller ice crystals, which reduces cell damage. This is why flash freezing is often used to preserve the quality of freshly caught seafood for the journey to your table. This is also done to all types of meat typically sold chilled in supermarkets, thawed ahead of time for the shopper's convenience.

Fortunately, this method is not limited to large manufacturers. You can also do rapid freezing at home without any special equipment. All you need is a freezer; fortunately, the freezer in your refrigerator will suffice most of the time.

Maintaining Quality When Freezing

You can take steps to ensure higher quality results when freezing, such as pre-treating produce, blanching, and preventing discoloration and freezer burn. Some items, for example, must be pre-treated to maintain their structure in cold temperatures. Similarly, most vegetables should be blanched before freezing, which can be accomplished by lightly steaming or boiling them. Blanching inhibits enzyme activity.

Some fruits, such as cut apples, darken when exposed to air. Apply one of three options to the fruit before freezing to prevent discoloration: lemon juice, salt water (2 teaspoons salt to 2 cups water), or a salt-vinegar solution (1 tablespoon salt + 1 tablespoon vinegar and 2 quarts water). This is especially important when working with lighter-colored fruits.

Freezer burn is another food-quality concern when it comes to freezing. Dehydration in frozen food is referred to as freezer burn. It may be found on the edges of frozen items where there is air exposure. It is not harmful but can affect the product's texture and flavor. Limiting the air to which a product is exposed by removing as much air as possible from the bags (vacuum sealing is ideal) or leaving only 12 inches of headspace in containers. Wrapping items tightly in aluminum foil or plastic wrap and taping them well also helps avoid freezer burn.

Tools and Equipment

Some of these are required (such as the freezer!) while others are optional.

Containers

Heavy-duty resealable plastic bags, plastic pint or quart containers, or other tougher plastic containers can be used. Many use "deli cups" from restaurant supply stores. It all depends on the size of the items you're storing and how efficiently these storage containers use the freezer space. Use heavy-duty foil and wrap it in plastic wrap to prevent tearing. And, as much as I love using glass for preservation projects, it is brittle.

Pack meat in appropriate containers. Different foods necessitate slightly different containers. Use caution when using large containers because they will cause the items to freeze slowly, which is counterintuitive to our goal. As a general rule, freezer containers should be food grade, moisture-proof, waterproof, durable, odorless, leakproof, and designed for the freezer. This means they should not crack or become brittle after prolonged use in the freezer.

Freezer-grade containers include plastic resealable freezer bags, rigid and resealable metal, glass, or plastic containers, and flexible or soft plastic/silicone containers. Carefully read the back labels of any containers you intend to purchase. They should be clearly labeled as freezer-safe. Most manufacturers would also include temperature limits for their products. Choose items that can withstand temperatures as low as 0°F.

Rigid containers hold liquids, soft foods, and easily broken down foods. The straight and hard sides make it simple to remove the food with a wet towel applied to the outside surface of the container. Most of them are also meant to nest or stack on top of one another. Metal and plastic are the most common materials used to make these containers. glass is another option; however, it should be noted that it has been tested for freezer use. Regular glass containers, such as canning jars can easily crack when temperatures drop below freezing. When using rigid containers, ensure the lids are tightly closed and airtight. If they are not, use freezer tape (tape designed for temperatures below freezing). Masking tapes should not be used because they may not adhere correctly.

The resealable plastic freezer bags and wraps that are widely available in stores are the most commonly used. Heavy-duty aluminum foil can also be used in a pinch. To avoid puncturing, keep them away from sharp objects and corners inside the freezer – using cardboard dividers in the freezer can protect the plastic wraps and aluminum foils. These bags are ideal for drier foods such as chops and steaks, as well as raw meat, fish, poultry, fruits, and vegetables.

Another container that has recently gained popularity on social media is the resealable silicone container, which can also be used as a freezer container. Because it is a hybrid of rigid, softer, more flexible wraps and bags, many people prefer it. Additionally, it is more durable than plastic freezer bags and is an environmentally friendly alternative to freezer bags.

Freezer

There are two types of freezers: upright and chest. Most of us are probably used to upright freezers. It is either a refrigerator/freezer combination or a stand-alone freezer. There are numerous size, style, and appearance variations. Because they are taller rather than wider, the uprights take up less space. However, these freezers are typically much smaller (especially when attached to a refrigerator) and lose cold air quickly when opened. If you need to do some serious freezing, chest freezers are ideal. They are larger and remain cold even when the door is opened because cool air tends to sink to the bottom. They do require more floor space. Whichever you choose, place it away from heat sources, such as your oven, and leave 2 to 4 inches between the back of the unit and the wall to allow for good airflow, which means the appliance won't have to work as hard to keep the temperature cold.

Ice-Cube Tray Made of Silicone

Although there is a long list of things that can be frozen in ice cube trays, you can also use these trays to portion out items that have a big impact in small doses, like lemon juice. Silicone ice cube trays are preferred because they make it easier to remove items from these trays.

Bags and Vacuum Sealer

A vacuum sealer machine removes all of the air from a specially designed bag; the bag conforms to a frozen item, cutting out oxygen. Simple sealers cost between $70 and $1,000 for commercial-grade sous vide sealers. Vacuum sealers are ideal for expensive items like meats and proteins because they ensure that as little air as possible comes into contact with the item, resulting in less freezer burn. This is also an excellent method for preparing single portions of large batch items; you can maximize storage space by eliminating unused space.

Freezing Meat at Home

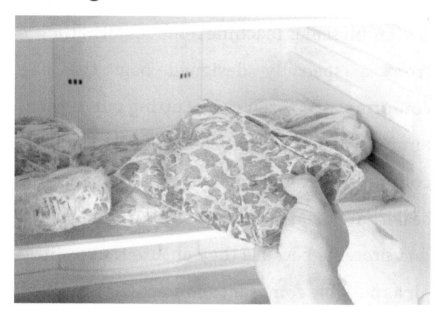

If you intend to freeze fresh meats at home, turn on the freezer and keep the temperature inside well below freezing – around -10°F or even lower – for a few hours ahead of time.

Meat that will be used within a week or so can be frozen in its original packaging; however, meat that will be stored for an extended period must be properly packaged and sealed. When storing meats for an ample time, keep them away from air and in an airtight or vacuum-sealed freezer bag to avoid freezer burn.

When working with fresh meats you have just brought home from the store, and you must work quickly and efficiently so that the meat does not have enough time to thaw while working thoroughly. Keep your countertop, hands, utensils, and equipment clean to avoid contamination. To prevent food poisoning, you must exercise extreme caution when handling raw poultry. Also, to keep your family safe, remember to clean and disinfect afterward.

To maintain the quality of the meat, the freezer temperature must be kept below 0°F even after the initial freeze is complete. Allowing food to be stored in a freezer at temperatures above 0°F may result in spoilage and shorter shelf life. Food that has been frozen should be kept frozen.

Place it in the coldest part of the freezer, usually against the walls. Take care not to crowd the area. Cramming your freezer with unfrozen food all at once will result in a slow freeze.

Red Meat

If you are a hunter or butcher, freezing your red meats may be the simplest and quickest thing you can do with them when you have a large quantity and have yet to find the time or the right recipe to make your summer sausage.

Most butchers and delis will gladly freeze your meat for you. It's ideal if you don't want to cook your meat immediately. Put them in the freezer when you get home.

Red meat can be frozen relatively easily. Simply keep them away from moisture and air to maintain their quality. Remove any excess fat and, if possible, all of the bones. It may arrive wrapped in plain butcher paper when you buy fresh meat from the butcher or the store. Meats wrapped in butcher paper or other paper wraps in the store cannot be relied on to prevent freezer burn.

If you don't intend to use them within a week of purchasing them, take them out and rewrap them in a freezer bag or a freezer-safe container. If you don't intend to remove the butcher paper, simply wrap them in a freezer-grade wrap or place them in a freezer-proof bag. Items purchased vacuum sealed and frozen, on the other hand, would require rewrapping. It's fine to refreeze them when you get home.

Furthermore, if you are storing or packing multiple individual cuts of meat in one package or container, place freezer paper or baking paper in between each piece to prevent them from freezing together for easier thawing. Tray packing smaller chunks of meat or cut pieces of poultry is also an option. Tray packing means freezing your meats in a baking tray, arranged, so they do not touch. Cover the tray with freezer-safe plastic wrap and place in the freezer until completely frozen. These can then be placed in smaller, more compact containers for easier storage.

Salted meats such as hams and luncheon meats should not be stored in the freezer even if they are already cured. You will notice that the salt in the cured meats causes your meat to go rancid faster. For other cured meats, such as hotdogs and luncheon meats, freezing temperatures cause the emulsions inside to break down and leak, causing the meat to "weep."

Lower temperatures will cause cooked meat to dry out much faster than raw meat. It is therefore strongly advised to store it in the sauce in which it was cooked. Submerge or coat your meats in gravy before sealing them in a bag or container. After thawing, your meats will retain their freshness while also becoming more flavorful from having had more time to absorb the sauce. However, remember that meats frozen in sauces or marinades will last much less time than fresh raw meat. Try to finish them within three months.

Poultry

When selecting poultry that is best for freezing, choose whole, fresh, and unblemished birds. To ensure freshness, choose plump and odorless ones. You can certainly buy poultry that has already been butchered, but it is well worth your time to learn how to cut up your poultry correctly. It is far easier than it appears and far easier than butchering beef or pork.

Pull and separate the legs and wings from the body before separating the thigh from the drumstick. Split the ribcage in half, separating the back from the breast. If desired, cut the breast in half to make smaller servings.

When selecting the right poultry to freeze, consider how you intend to cook it. Choose more flavorful birds if you want to cook stews. Young poultry, on the other hand, is ideal for roasting and frying.

Before freezing your poultry, prepare it according to how you intend to use it in the future. Birds cut up for specific recipes must be chopped up before freezing. The same is true for cooked birds in half or whole. However, the stuffing inside stuffed poultry should not be frozen. The stuffing is more likely to contain toxic bacteria during thawing and refreezing. The filling can be frozen separately from the poultry. The giblets, gizzard, heart, liver, and neck should also be packed separately because they spoil faster, in about two weeks. These are excellent for making gravy or stuffing.

Pack chopped-up birds in the same manner as you would other red meats. Place freezer paper between individual portions to make separation easier when taking them out. You can also tray individual pack pieces of poultry, which, like red meats, come wrapped in butcher paper when purchased fresh from butcher shops and stores. These papers will not keep your birds from getting burned in the freezer. If you intend to keep these birds in your freezer for more than a week, rewrap or overwrap them until they arrive vacuum-sealed. If they are, do not open them; simply place them in the freezer.

Fish

Fish is much more challenging to prepare than red meat because it spoils quickly. If you catch them fresh, in addition to gutting, descaling, and cleaning them, you should also salt them or dunk them in an ascorbic acid solution to improve their shelf life. So, if you buy them from a fishmonger, ask them to gut, clean, and descale the fish. This will speed up your freezing preparation when you get home.

Freshly caught fish must be frozen immediately, so if you're out on the lake and don't plan on returning home soon, keep your fish packed deep within a large cooler filled with crushed ice. When you get home, thoroughly wash the fish in fresh potable water, then descale it by gently running the back of your knife back and forth against the skin. To remove the entrails, cut the fish's belly. When cutting, be careful not to puncture the innards, as this will impart a bitter taste to your fish. Remove the fish's head and rinse everything in fresh potable water again, paying particular attention to the fish's stomach cavity.

The back and dorsal fins are then removed with a sharp knife. Cut from the base, not leaving any fin stumps in the fish. To remove all the fins cleanly, cut along the side of the fish. Rinse the fish in water once more. After taking larger fish out of the freezer, it is recommended that they be chopped up or filleted for easier cooking. Larger fish, such as tuna or salmon, and large Spanish mackerels, should be cut into 34-inch-thick crosswise steaks.

Cut the back of a medium-sized fish, from the collarbone to the tail, to fillet it. Make another cut along the fish's tail, flattening the knife and slicing the flesh off, running the knife along the spine from the tail to the collarbone. Flip the fish over and repeat the procedure on the other side. Feel for fish bones stuck inside the flesh by running the back of your knife along the fish's spine. Pull out all of the fish bones with a tweezer.

To improve the quality of the fish, pre-treat it before freezing. This will reduce rancidity and the likelihood of flavor change. Dip fish with high-fat content, such as tuna, salmon, mackerel, trout, and mullet, in an ascorbic acid solution for 20 to 30 seconds.

To make the solution, combine two teaspoons of crystalline ascorbic acid and one quart of fresh potable water. Immerse lean fish like snapper, grouper, flounder, cod, croaker, redfish, whiting, and most freshwater species like bass, catfish, and crappie in brine for 20 to 30 seconds. The brine solution combines 14 cups of salt and 1 quart of fresh and cold potable water. This solution will firm the flesh and reduce drip loss when thawing the fish.

After pre-treatment, you have three options for freezing fish. The most convenient method is to wrap it in freezer wrap or place it in a freezer bag. Remove the air from the bag and place it directly in the freezer. For easier thawing, place freezer paper or baking paper between individual slices before freezing, just as you would with individual pieces of meat and poultry.

You can also put it in a rigid container and cover it with fresh potable water before freezing it. Cover the container tightly with an airtight lid or freezer-safe wrap after covering all parts of the fish with water.

You can also use the ice glaze method. This method is primarily used with vacuum-packed, frozen fish commonly found in supermarkets. To do this, unwrap and separate the fish (whole, cut, or filleted) in a tray and freeze. Once completely frozen, quickly immerse the fish or individual pieces of it in very cold, fresh potable water, then place it back in the freezer. Dunk and refreeze the fish several times until a uniform and visible layer of hard ice coats it. This will form a thin layer of water on the fish's surface, protecting it from the harsh environment of the freezer. Afterward, place the ice-glazed fish in a freezer bag and freeze it. Also, keep individual pieces separate from one another.

Fish roe, a delicacy in and of itself, should be frozen separately. Roe is the most perishable part of the fish and should be carefully removed from the stomach cavity and thoroughly washed with fresh potable water. To prepare the egg sacs for freezing, pierce them in several places with a clean and disinfected needle, then dunk them in an ascorbic acid solution like you would with fatty fish. A dip of 20 to 30 seconds would suffice. This will also reduce the rancidity and flavor change effect on the fish eggs when stored in the freezer. After that, freeze the egg sacs in individual freezer wraps or bags. Remember to use up the roe within three months.

Game

To prevent spoilage when storing fresh-caught wild game in the freezer, field dress and process large animals such as deer, antelope, and moose. As with other red meats, butcher and clean the meat before freezing it. Remove the bloodshot meat and discard it before freezing the meat. This will spoil faster and should be thrown away.

Squirrels and rabbits, for example, should be skinned, dressed, and refrigerated or chilled as soon as possible after being killed. Refrigerate it for a day or two until the meat is pliable and no longer rigid. Prepare or cut the meat as you intend to cook it in the future—pack and freeze as you would any other red meat.

Duck, geese, dove, quail, and pheasant should be bled, plucked of feathers, gutted, cleaned, and refrigerated or chilled immediately after shooting. Remember to trim or cut off any excess fat to prevent rancidity, especially on geese and ducks. Pack and freeze these game birds in the same manner as you would other poultry.

Thawing

To avoid the growth of bacteria that can cause spoilage, it is strongly advised to thaw meat, fish, and poultry in the refrigerator. Meats such as steaks and other large cuts of meat and whole poultry should be partially thawed before being placed in a pot or oven to cook. Larger pieces of meat and poultry can be partially thawed to avoid being overdone on the outside and undercooked or raw on the inside.

Frozen meats, fish, and poultry that will be breaded or battered before cooking, on the other hand, should be partially thawed so that the breading batter adheres to the surface. It is preferable to thaw frozen food before completely deep-frying it. Because of the high heat and short cooking time, the outside will be cooked quickly while the inside or center will remain frozen.

Cooking frozen meat takes a long time and should be done slowly over low heat. Cooking at high temperatures results in unbalanced cooking: the surface will char or cook quickly, but the inside will remain cold and frozen. If this is possible with chilled or refrigerated items, the likelihood of serving a charred but frozen inside roast with frozen meats is higher. Depending on the size of the cuts, frozen food will generally take half or twice the time that chilled or room temperature meat, fish, or poultry would.

There are three methods for thawing meats, poultry, and fish straight from the freezer. The quickest and safest method would be to thaw the sealed packages in the refrigerator. Place it on a tray or other container to catch drippings and keep meltwater from flooding your fridge. Smaller cuts will, of course, thaw much faster, taking only a few hours, but larger whole birds and larger cuts of meat may take a day or more to defrost thoroughly.

Submerging the sealed package in a bowl of room temperature water is an old method for thawing or defrosting frozen food. Replace the water every half hour until the item is completely defrosted. To avoid spoilage, the items must be cooked immediately after being thawed using this method.

When you buy microwaves, many of them come with a defrost function. As long as they fit inside the oven, these can also be used to defrost meats, fish, and poultry. You may need to turn and flip the items while defrosting to ensure that everything thaws evenly. Food defrosted in the microwave must be cooked immediately after defrosting, like food defrosted by submerging it in water.

Frozen meats, fish, and poultry should never be left to defrost at room temperature. This causes the bacteria to multiply rapidly, contaminating your food.

Before defrosted raw food items can be safely frozen again, they must be completely defrosted and cooked. Thawing or defrosting and then freezing again will result in larger ice crystals than desired. The meat's cell walls will rupture, causing the meat's quality to deteriorate over time. Cook them after defrosting to reduce moisture, flavor, and quality loss before freezing them again. However, it is perfectly safe to defrost an item inside the refrigerator and then change your mind and need to freeze it again. However, doing so will reduce the quality of the meat.

Flash Freezing

Individual food portions should be flash-frozen in a single layer on a parchment-lined tray to allow for easy separation. For easier storage, place the frozen items in heavy-duty resealable plastic bags. The following are the best flash freeze items:

- Avocado
- Banana
- Snap or shelled beans
- Berries
- Coconut
- Kernels of corn
- Flours
- Grains (raw and cooked)
- Seeds and nuts
- Shelled peas
- Stone fruits

The greater the surface area of an item, the greater its exposure to the elements and the shorter its storage time. A cut of meat, for example, will keep longer than ground beef. Similarly, preparing animal proteins before freezing reduces storage time compared to freezing them in their raw state. Foods with a high-fat content will also have a shorter storage life.

Beans and grains don't have their section here, but that doesn't mean they can't be frozen. On the contrary, they are excellent for freezing. The rules are the same regardless of the type of cooking. Cooked grains can be flash-frozen by spreading them on a parchment-lined baking sheet and freezing them. Transfer to a labeled heavy-duty resealable plastic bag once frozen. Freeze beans in their cooking liquid in a pint or quart-size container or flat in a bag in the same manner. They will keep in the freezer for six months. Thaw in the refrigerator overnight, microwave, or reheat on the stovetop in a covered container over low heat.

Meat, Poultry, and Proteins

Thaw meats and proteins in the fridge for best quality—this could take overnight or several days, depending on the size of the pieces. Some frozen items, such as dinners and casseroles, can be cooked directly from the freezer. You can also place the meat in its wrapping in a bowl of cool water on the counter, changing the water frequently to keep it cool. Alternatively, you can thaw in the microwave at 50% power, but check it often so it doesn't start to cook.

Item	Months To Keep Frozen
Bacon and sausage	1 to 2
Casseroles	2 to 3
Egg whites or egg substitute	12
Frozen dinners and entrées	3 to 4
Gravy, meat, or poultry	2 to 3

Ham, hot dogs, lunch meats	1 to 2
Meat, cooked	2 to 3
Meat, uncooked ground	3 to 4
Meat, uncooked roasts	4 to 12
Meat, uncooked steaks, or chops	4 to 12
Poultry, cooked	4
Poultry, uncooked giblets	3 to 4
Poultry, uncooked parts	9
Poultry, uncooked whole	12
Soups and stews	2 to 3
Wild game, uncooked	8 to 12

Fruits

Many fruits can be flash-frozen and then kept frozen, but some foods benefit from pre-treatment. All of these fruits will keep in the freezer for nine months to a year in general but check them periodically to ensure they aren't developing freezer burn and that the packaging is still intact. You can use these straight from the freezer for baking or smoothies or heat them up for sauces and compotes. Fruit that has been frozen can also be a tasty and refreshing snack. Remember that their texture will be softer than fresh fruits, so choose a cooking method that considers this.

Type of Food	Prep Notes
Apples	Peel, core, slice, and dip into acidulated water; can sprinkle with sugar or turn into applesauce
Apricots	Pit; ascorbic acid dip; sugar sprinkle (optional); can puree
Bananas	Peel and slice; ascorbic acid dip; can mash
Blueberries	Blanch for 30 seconds for a firm texture; sugar sprinkle for a soft texture; can crush/puree
Cherries	Stem and pit; sugar sprinkle

Citrus	Peel, segment, or pull apart; sugar sprinkle (optional); can juice
Cranberries	Blanch for 30 seconds for a firm texture; sugar sprinkle for a soft texture; can crush/puree
Figs	Peel (optional); sugar sprinkle (optional); can crush
Grapes	Sugar sprinkle (optional); can juice
Guava	Peel and cut; sugar sprinkle (optional); can puree (add lemon juice)
Loquats	Cut and seed; acidulated water; can puree (add juice)
Mango	Peel and slice; sugar sprinkle (optional); can puree
Melons	Peel, remove soft areas, cube, slice, or ball; sugar sprinkle (optional); can crush (add lemon juice)
Peaches and nectarines	Peel, pit, and slice; acidulated water dip; sugar dip; can crush/puree
Pears	Peel, core, and slice; acidulated water dip; sugar sprinkle (optional); can puree

Persimmons	Peel and cut; can puree (add juice)
Pineapple	Peel, remove eyes/core; dice or slice; sugar sprinkle (optional); can crush
Plums	Cut and pit; acidulated water dip; sugar dip; can puree (use juice)
Rhubarb	Cut into 1-to 2-inch pieces; blanch for 1 minute; sugar sprinkle (optional); can puree (cook in boiling water)

Vegetables

Most vegetables must be pre-treated in some way before freezing. Vegetables can be stored in the freezer for nine months to a year, but check them regularly to ensure they don't develop freezer burn and that the packaging is still intact. For a quick side dish, stir into casseroles, roast straight from the freezer, or heat on the stovetop or microwave. Like fresh fruit, the texture of vegetables will be softer than when cooked, so use a cooking method that takes this into account.

Type of Food	Prep Notes
Asparagus	Trim and blanch
Beets	Roast or boil until thoroughly cooked; peel. If small, freeze whole, or quarter and flash freeze
Broccoli and cauliflower	Separate florets, chop stems, blanch
Broccoli rabe	Trim, chop, and blanch
Brussels sprouts	Halve large sprouts, keep small ones whole; blanch
Carrots	Slice or chop; blanch
Celery	Slice or chop
Corn	Blanch on the cob, then cut off kernels
Eggplant	Slice or halve (if small), salt for 30 minutes, then roast until tender

Fennel bulb	Core, slice, and roast until tender, or chop and freeze (the texture will suffer if you don't pre-cook, so this is appropriate for soups and casseroles)
Garlic	Roast whole, then puree or mash the cloves; freeze in ice-cube trays
Ginger	Grate or juice and freeze in ice-cube trays, or freeze, whole and unpeeled, in plastic wrap—to use, grate from frozen
Green beans	Trim and blanch
Hardy greens	Sauté, cool, and freeze in a heavy-duty resealable plastic bag
Herbs	Blend with water or oil and freeze in ice-cube trays
Leeks	Slice or chop
Mushrooms	Slice or chop, dip in acidulated water, then steam blanch, sauté, or roast
Okra	Trim and blanch
Onions and shallots	Slice or chop
Parsnips	Slice or chop, then blanch

Peppers, sweet and hot	Slice, chop, or leave whole if small; can roast before freezing
Potatoes	Peel, chop, blanch, or roast (do not need to cook fully)
Scallions	Puree or finely chop, mix with water or oil; freeze in ice-cube trays
Spinach and other tender greens	Sauté, cool, and freeze in a heavy-duty resealable plastic bag
Squash, summer	Slice ½ inch thick and blanch
Squash, winter	Roast and mash, or cube and blanch until fully cooked
Sweet potatoes	Peel, chop, blanch, or roast (do not need to cook fully)
Tomatillos	Remove husks, score, freeze whole or roast and freeze
Tomatoes	Blanch and peel, or freeze whole or chopped, or roast and freeze

Troubleshooting

Issue	Root Cause	Solution	Keep/Toss
The surface of food is light-colored; food is tough or dried out	Freezer burn; food exposed to air	• Seal food tightly, making sure there are no tears/rips • Use vacuum-seal bags • Remove as much air as possible from the bag	Keep, but taste and consistency will be altered
Brownish color in vegetables	No blanching	Blanch vegetables before freezing	Keep, but taste and consistency will be altered

Food is mushy	• Freez er burn; food exposed to air • Tem peratur e fluctuat ion • Food too large or dense when frozen	• Seal food tightly, making sure there are no tears/rips • Use vacuum-seal bags • Remove as much air as possible from the bag • Freeze foods at 0°F or below and maintain the temperature during storage • Freeze smaller portions	Toss
Watery/g ummy consisten cy in fruits	• Freez er burn; food exposed to air	• Seal food tightly, making sure there are no tears/rips	Toss

	• Temperature fluctuation Food too large or dense when frozen	• Use vacuum-seal bags • Remove as much air as possible from the bag • Freeze foods at 0°F or below and maintain the temperature during storage • Freeze smaller portions	
Discoloration in fruits	No pre-treatment	Light-colored fruits need to be treated in sugar syrup or citric acid.	Safe, but the taste and appearance will be altered

How to Properly Store Frozen Food

Although frozen food can be stored for long periods, its quality and nutrition degrade over time. Even though food can be stored in the freezer indefinitely, don't try to keep it for 50,000 years. Eating beef sitting in the back of your freezer for over a decade is still dangerous. Here's a convenient list that shows how long food can be kept in the freezer.

Seafood

- 2 to 3 months for fatty fish (perch, salmon, and mackerel).
- 3 to 6 months for lean fish (flounder, cod, and sole).
- 4 to 6 months for cooked fish
- 2 months for smoked fish (sealed and vacuum-packed)
- 3 to 6 months for shellfish (e.g., mussels, oysters, scallops)
- 3 to 5 months for shrimp
- 2 months for cooked crab

Processed Meat

- 1 to 2 months for bacon
- 1 to 2 months for luncheon meat (open/sealed package or deli-sliced)

- 3 to 4 months for burgers and ground meat patties (beef, pork, poultry, veal, lamb, and other meats)
- 1 to 2 months for (opened or sealed) hot dogs
- 1 to 2 months for raw sausages (made from beef, chicken, pork, or turkey)
- 1 to 2 months for cooked sausages (made from beef, chicken, pork, or turkey)
- 2 months of pre-frozen sausages (made from beef, chicken, pork, or turkey)
- 5 to 6 months for fresh ham, uncooked and uncured
- 3 to 4 months for fresh ham, cooked and uncured
- 1 to 2 months for fresh ham cured, cooked, and vacuum sealed (unopened)
- 1 month for country ham

- Canned and unopened (labeled "keep refrigerated"): no need to freeze; it will last 6 to 9 months in the fridge
- 1 to 2 months if canned and opened (shelf-stable)
- 1 month for Italian and Spanish hams (Parma, Prosciutto, Serrano, and so on)
- 2 to 3 months for lamb and beef fresh ground meat
- 1 to 2 months for pork fresh ground meat
- 6 to 12 months for beef slices, fresh whole (for steaks and chops)
- 3 to 6 months for pork slices, fresh whole (for steaks and chops)
- 1 to 2 months for veal and lamb slices, fresh whole (for steaks and chops)
- 6 to 12 months for fresh beef (for roasts)
- 3 to 6 months for fresh pork (for roasts)

- 6 to 9 months for fresh lamb and veal (for roasts)

Poultry

- 12 months for a whole chicken
- 6 months for chopped or cut chicken
- 12 months for a whole turkey
- 6 months for chopped or cut turkey
- 6 months for an entire goose and duck
- 3 months for giblets
- 8 to 12 months for uncooked wild game

Pre-Cooked and Cooked Food

- 3 months for stews or casseroles (meat, poultry, and fish)
- 3 months for meat pies
- 8 months for fruit pies (unbaked)
- 2 to 4 months for baked fruit pies
- 3 months for bread
- 3 months for the cake

- 3 months for cookies (baked and unbaked)
- 6 to 9 months for dairy butter
- 12 months for margarine
- 1 month for fresh milk
- 2 months for heavy cream
- 1 month for whipped cream
- 2 months for ice cream
- 5 to 8 weeks for organic and natural cheeses
- 4 months for processed cheeses

Eggs

- 12 months for raw beaten eggs (raw eggs keep better in the freezer when beaten)
- 12 months for Raw eggs (in shells); however, keep refrigerated until thawed.

Overall, food appropriately stored in subzero temperatures will keep you going for a long time, if not indefinitely, but be careful if the frozen item has been sleeping in the back of a freezer for years. Avoid eating food that appears and smells off or rotten to avoid food poisoning.

Chapter 3:

Recipes to Help You Get Started with Your Freeze-Drying Process

Teriyaki Marinade

Preparation Time: 10 minutes

Cooking Time: 35 minutes

Makes: 1 cup

Ingredients:

- ⅓ c. soy sauce
- ⅓ c. rice wine vinegar
- 3 tbsp. olive oil
- 2 tbsp. light brown sugar
- 1 tsp. thinly sliced garlic or ½ teaspoon garlic powder
- 1 tsp. grated peeled fresh ginger or ½ teaspoon ground ginger

Directions:

1. In a medium bowl, large measuring cup, or jar, combine the soy sauce, vinegar, oil,

sugar, garlic, and ginger. Whisk well to combine.

2. If you are freezing the marinade alone, pour it into a plastic pint container, or freeze flat in a heavy-duty resealable plastic bag.

3. If you are freezing the marinade with chicken, tofu, or tempeh, place the protein in a vacuum or heavy-duty resealable plastic bag. Pour the marinade into the bag. Close the bag, removing as much air as possible.

4. Place the bag on a flat dish in the freezer for 3 hours or until frozen solid. Check the bag to ensure there are no leaks—label and use within three months.

Tomato Paste

Preparation Time: 30 minutes, plus 1 hour to cool

Cooking Time: 4 to 26 hours

Makes: 4 half-pints or 32 ice cubes

Ingredients:

- 12 lbs. tomatoes, cored and chopped (4 quarts); if you don't have a food mill, blanch and peel the tomatoes before coring and chopping
- 2 bay leaves
- ½ tsp. Diamond Crystal kosher salt (optional)

Directions:

1. If using a food mill, skip this step. In a large pot over high heat, cook the chopped tomatoes for 30 minutes, stirring frequently and crushing them with a

wooden spoon to break them down and make them soft. Press the cooked tomatoes through a fine-mesh sieve into a slow cooker.

2. If using a food mill, pass the raw tomatoes through a food mill into a slow cooker.

3. Add the bay leaves to the cooker, cover the cooker, and cook on high heat for 2 hours. After 2 hours, the puree should be bubbling.

4. Turn the lid slightly to the side so there is an opening for air to escape, or use two wooden spoons to prop up the lid. The objective is to have air flowing out of the cooker while keeping the puree hot so it can reduce. Cook for 24 hours, checking it and stirring every so often. The paste is ready when it holds its shape on a spoon.

5. Alternatively, place the puree in a saucepan, add the bay leaves, and place the pan over medium heat. Cook for 1½ to 2 hours, frequently stirring to avoid burning. When the paste is thick and coats the spoon, remove it from the heat and let it cool for 1 hour.

6. Taste the paste; add the salt if using.

7. Once cooled, remove the bay leaves from the paste, spoon the paste into an ice-cube tray, and freeze for 1 hour.

8. Transfer the cubes into a heavy-duty resealable plastic bag when the paste is frozen. Keep frozen, labeled, for up to 6 months. If you have vacuum-sealer bags, portion the cubes into groups of 4 and vacuum seal the bags for freezing.

Chicken Bone Broth

Preparation Time: 15 minutes

Cooking Time: 8 hours 30 minutes (stovetop);
15 hours 30 minutes (slow cooker)

Makes: 4 quarts

Ingredients:

- 20 c. water
- Bones from 1 whole roasted chicken, picked clean of meat
- 1 yellow onion, quartered
- 1 celery stalk halved
- 3 carrots, roughly chopped
- 3 garlic cloves, peeled
- 1 bay leaf
- 2 tsp. Diamond Crystal kosher salt (optional), divided, plus more as needed

Directions:

1. In a slow cooker, combine the water, bones, onion, celery, carrots, garlic, bay leaf, and one teaspoon of salt (if using). Cover the cooker and cook on high heat for 10 to 15 minutes until the liquid starts to boil. If 20 cups of water are too much for your slow cooker, just cover the bones with water.

2. Once the broth boils, turn the slow cooker temperature to low. If you are making this on the stovetop, combine the ingredients in a large stockpot over high heat and bring it to a boil. Reduce the heat to low, partially cover the pot with a lid, and simmer for 6 to 8 hours. With either appliance, maintain a simmer or low boil.

3. Check the broth at the 5-hour mark. You should start to see the chicken fat on the top of the broth and the vegetables softening.

4. After the 10-hour mark, the broth will start to become ready. The chicken bones should be brittle, and you can crush them easily.

5. By hour 15, the vegetables will almost disintegrate upon touching them. Taste the broth and turn off the heat.

6. Using a fine-mesh strainer set over a large heatproof bowl, filter out all the bones and vegetables from the broth. Taste the broth. Add the remaining teaspoon of salt (if used), stir, and taste again. If you need more salt, add it to taste.

7. Pour the broth into four quart-size plastic containers, leaving 1½ inches of

headspace to allow the broth to expand while freezing—freeze, labeled, for up to 6 months.

Spinach and Parmesan Frittatas

Preparation Time: 15 minutes

Cooking Time: 35 minutes

Makes: 12 frittatas

Ingredients:

- 2 tbsp. olive oil or butter, divided
- 1 c. chopped onion
- 1 (16-ounce) package frozen spinach, thawed, squeezed dry, and chopped
- 12 large eggs
- ½ tsp. Diamond Crystal kosher salt
- ½ tsp. freshly ground black pepper
- ¾ c. grated parmesan cheese
- 1 tbsp. dried parsley or dill (optional)

Directions:

1. Preheat the oven to 350°F. Coat a 12-cup muffin tin, or two 6-cup tins, using one tablespoon of oil.

2. Heat the remaining one tablespoon of oil over medium heat in a small skillet. Add the onion and cook for about 8 minutes, stirring, until soft.

3. Add the spinach and cook for 2 minutes, just until hot. Evenly distribute the vegetable mixture among the prepared cups.

4. Whisk the eggs, salt, and pepper in a large bowl until blended. Whisk in the cheese and dried herbs, if desired.

5. Pour the egg mixture into a large measuring cup and evenly distribute it into the muffin tin, using all the custard.

6. Bake for 25 minutes until the eggs are lightly browned on the top and sizzling on the sides.

7. Let cool to room temperature. Remove the cooled frittatas from the tin and place them into a heavy-duty resealable plastic bag—freeze, labeled, for up to 3 months.

8. To reheat, microwave on high power for 2 minutes.

Vegan Soup

Preparation Time: 20 minutes

Cooking Time: 30 minutes

Makes: 1 cup

Ingredients:

- 4 tbsp. of olive oil
- 2 c. chopped leeks, white part only (from approximately three medium leeks)

- 2 tbsp. finely minced garlic, Kosher salt
- 2 c. carrots, peeled and chopped into rounds (about two medium)
- 2 c. peeled and diced potatoes
- 2 c. fresh green beans, broken or cut into 3/4-inch pieces
- 2 qt. of chicken or vegetable broth
- 4 c. peeled, seeded, and chopped tomatoes
- 2 ears of corn, kernels removed
- ½ tsp. freshly ground black pepper
- ¼ c. packed, chopped fresh parsley leaves
- 1 to 2 tsp. freshly squeezed lemon juice

Directions:

1. In a sizable, heavy-bottomed stockpot, warm the olive oil over medium-low heat.
2. Once hot, add the leeks, garlic, and a dash of salt, and cook for 7 to 8 minutes, or until they start to soften.

3. Stirring occasionally, add the carrots, potatoes, and green beans. Cook for 4 to 5 minutes.

4. Add the stock, increase the heat to high, and bring to a simmer. Once simmering, add the tomatoes, corn kernels, and pepper.

5. Reduce the heat to low, cover, and cook until the vegetables are fork-tender, approximately 25 to 30 minutes.

6. Remove from heat and add the parsley and lemon juice—season to taste with kosher salt. Serve immediately.

Conclusion

Thank you for taking the time to read this book. Almost any food can be freeze-dried, though some perform better than others. The meat you intend to freeze-dry should be cut up into smaller chunks to be more suitable for this method, as smaller-sized food will fare better. Coffee, soups, and other liquids fare well after freeze-drying as well. Most of the instant coffees we consume daily to keep us awake, and alert are either freeze-dried or spray-dried. Freeze-dried fruits and vegetables are becoming more popular in stores as healthier alternatives to dehydrated foods.

A freeze-drying machine is costly. One machine will cost you between $2000 and $4000. On the bright side, if you only freeze-dry a small amount of food each year, you don't need to spend that much.

A deep freezer is more efficient and will speed up the process, as a standard freezer will take weeks to complete. Neither method works well with meat, which is difficult to store.

Before freezing food, make sure it is clean and dry. Remove any dirt or moisture from the items, and cut all food into uniform chunks to ensure consistency. Bread, cakes, and other yeast-based products should not be frozen because they will change color when reconstituted.

The best time to freeze-dry food is when it is cold, and you have cooled it off. If you're making a complete meal, freeze-dry it as soon as you're done cooking it. Then, when recondensing, you'll need to test the results with a thermometer.

Good luck and have fun!

Made in the USA
Middletown, DE
28 July 2022